Italy

Children's travel activity book and journal

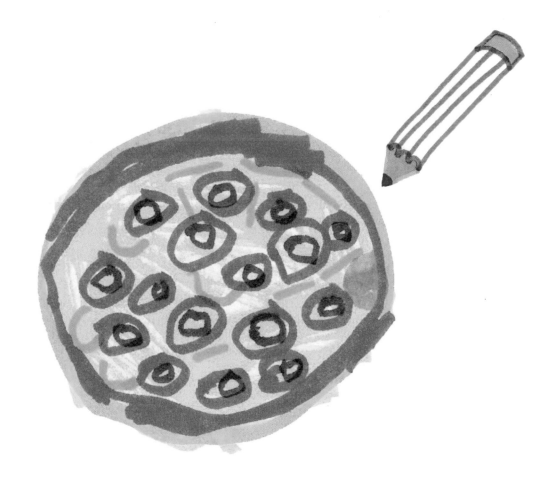

tinytourists

explore. discover. learn.

Hello!

My name's Topher*
and I love adventures!

I'll be keeping you company on your journey through this book. Look out for me, I'll be popping up every now and again.

Count how many times you can spot me...I'm quite good at hiding...

*Topher is named after St. Christ**opher**, the patron saint for travellers who is known for keeping all those who travel safe from harm. Check out his story on our website plus free activity sheets on keeping safe on holiday and how to be a responsible tiny tourist: www.tinytourists.co.uk

tinytourists is all about inspiring family travel and making the most of adventures; keeping travel meaningful and memorable, educational and fun. Visit us on Facebook to find out more and to join the tinytourists' community.

· ·

Written and Designed by Louise Amodio
Illustrated by Louise Amodio and Catherine Mantle
Cover Illustration by Giacomo (age 7)

Published by Beans and Joy Publishing Ltd as a product from Tiny Tourists Ltd, Great Britain.
www.beansandjoy.com

ISBN: 978-1-912293-05-6

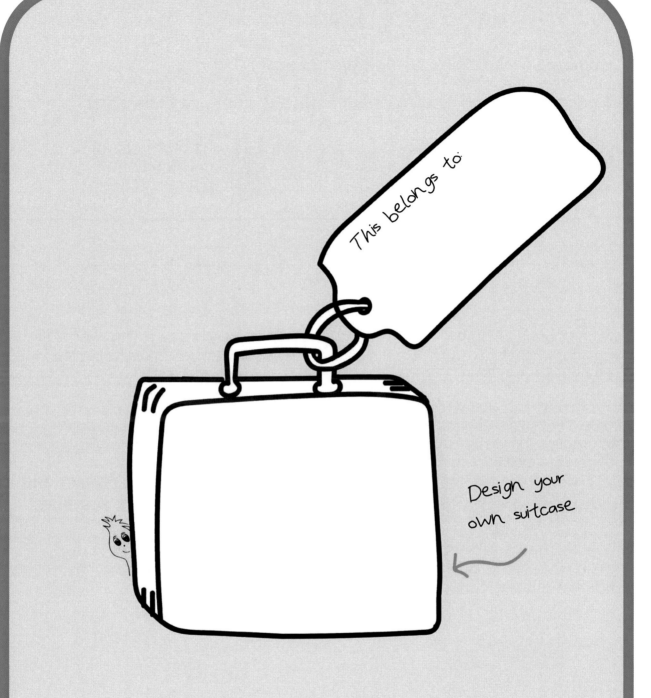

This belongs to:

Design your own suitcase

How to use this book

Welcome to your fabulously fun-packed Italy activity book!

Look out for these symbols to tell you what type of activity you'll be doing:

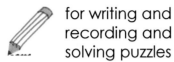 for writing and recording and solving puzzles

 for drawing and colouring and being creative

Time to get started!

Section 1: My Travel Log

Show off your planning skills; when you are going, where you are going, who you're going with, what the weather be like, and what you'll pack in your suitcase. This will help form part of a lovely keepsake as well as get you organised!

Section 2: Epic Explorer Skills

Time for some fun - full of games and activities for a bit of Italy-themed fun, as well as practice your extraordinary explorer skills;

PROBLEM-SOLVING (MATHS), CODE-BREAKING AND COMMUNICATING (LITERACY AND LANGUAGES) AND SPY SKILLS (SCIENCE AND GEOGRAPHY). SEE INDEX FOR INFO.

Want to learn some Italian words too? Look out for some new words you can practice while you're on your trip. We give you the real Italian spelling and how they sound phonetically too. Have a practice with these three important words:

phrase: ciao
say: (chow)
meaning: hello

phrase: grazie
say: (grazi-eh)
meaning: thank you

phrase: por favor
say: (poor fav-or)
meaning: please

Section 3: Memory Bank

This is where you can record all the memories from your trip. The perfect finishing touch to a lovely book of holiday memories; what you did, what you ate, what you saw, what you collected, and fun lists for recording the best bits and the worst bits.

Buon Viaggio!

My Info

Me:

My home address:

Eye Colour:

Hair Colour:

How long is your right index finger?

Distinguishing features:

0 1 2 3 4 5 6 7 8 9 10 11 12 13 14 15 16 cm

My Destination:

Arrival:

Date: _____

Passport Stamp:

Departure:

Date: _____

Where am I going?

Can you mark with an X where you're going in Italy on this map?

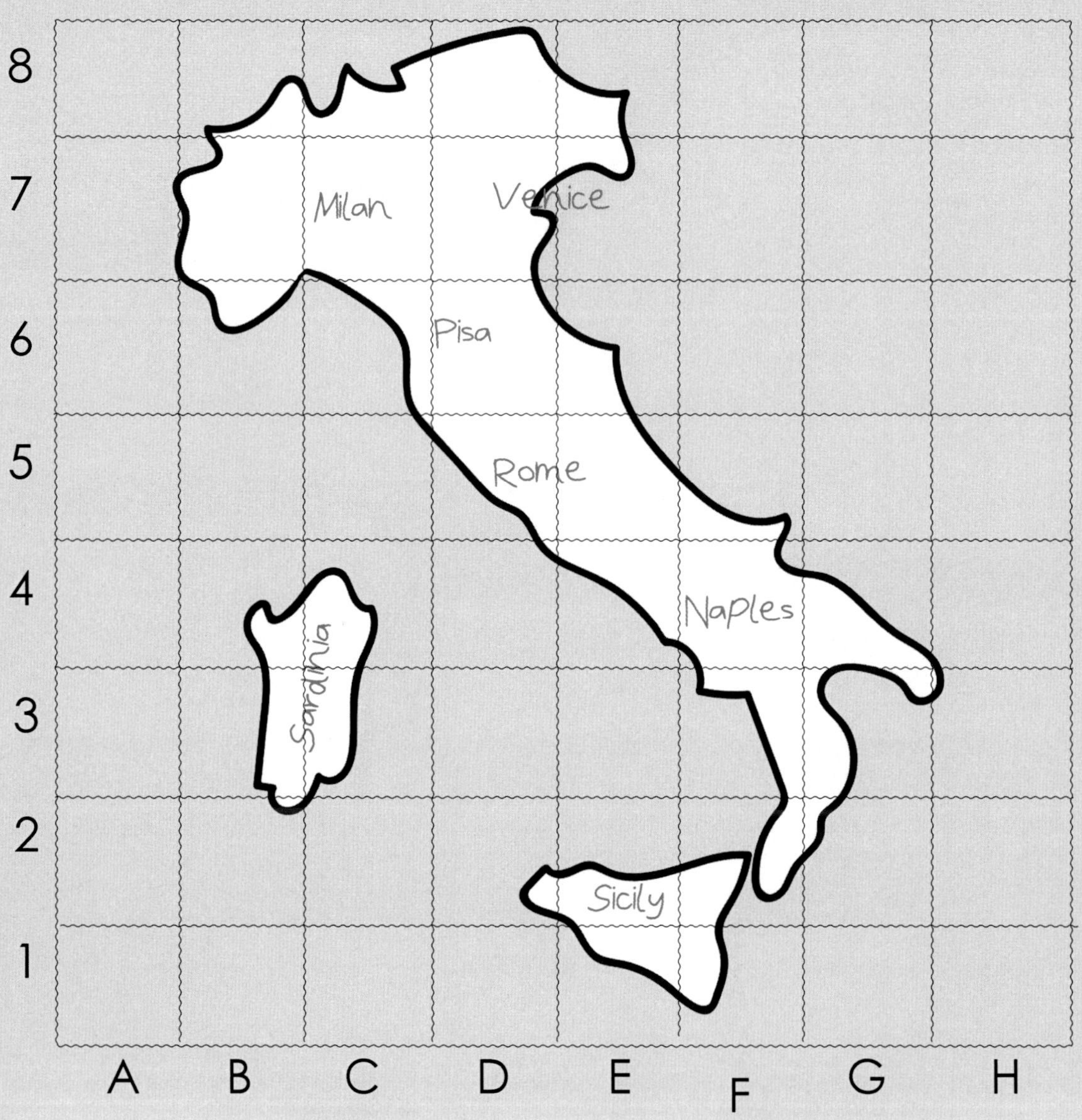
8
7
6
5
4
3
2
1
Milan
Venice
Pisa
Rome
Naples
Sardinia
Sicily
A
B
C
D
E
F
G
H

Can you find the grid codes for each of these places in Italy?

Milan: C7 Pisa: Rome: Naples:

Where are you staying?

How will I get there?

For each type of transport you use to get to Italy,
how many hours will you spend? Add it all up for the grand total:

	Hours
L'airplane (lair plan-eh)	
Il autobus (eel ow-toe bus)	
La macchina (la maki-na)	
Il treno (eel tren-o)	
La barca (la barka)	
Total:	

What am I taking with me?

Can you write or draw 6 things you want to pack in your bag?

~~~~~~~~~~~~~~~~~~~~   ~~~~~~~~~~~~~~~~~~~~   ~~~~~~~~~~~~~~~~~~~~

~~~~~~~~~~~~~~~~~~~~   ~~~~~~~~~~~~~~~~~~~~   ~~~~~~~~~~~~~~~~~~~~

Who am I going with?

Draw a picture of who you're going on holiday with in the frame below:

Can you learn their names in Italian?

Example

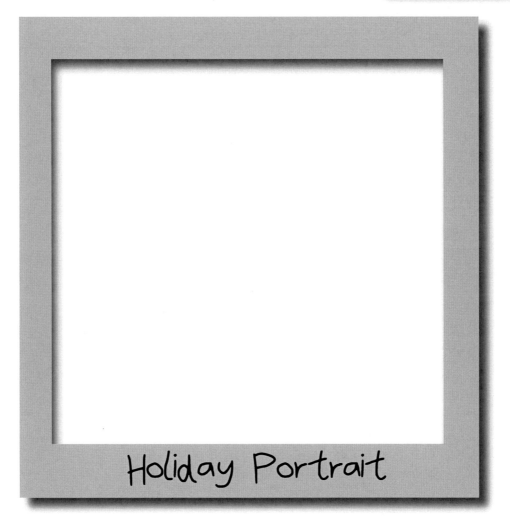

Holiday Portrait

La mia mama
(eel mia mamo)
My mummy

Il mio papa *(eel mio papa)*
My daddy

Il mio fratello
(il mio fratelo)
My brother

La mia sorella
(la mia sorela)
My sister

What will the weather be like?

Draw a circle around the weather you predict you'll have, and then record the actual weather you really do have:

Piove
(pee-of-ay)
It's raining

C'e il sole
(che il solay)
It's sunny

Sta nevicando
(sta nevi cando)
It's snowing

What weather DID you have?
Was your prediction correct?

Epic Explorer Skills

PROBLEM-SOLVING (MATHS)

CODE-BREAKING & COMMS (LITERACY & LANGUAGES)

SPY SKILLS (SCIENCE, GEOGRAPHY)

Il Tricolore

This is the Italian flag, with 3 colours, green, white and red.

How many flags can you spot on your travels?

Colour in this flag

verde
(vair-de)
green

bianco
(bee-anco)
white

rosso
(ross-o)
red

12

Ferrari, Olives, Pizza...
Can you find these famous Italian objects in the wordsearch?

Wordsearch

```
P I Z W D R R E F X
L O I G R A P E S X
P O M O D O R O V G
O L P O M R W L O E
P I Z Z A X U P L L
S V E R I S R U C A
C E I C H D R I A T
O S M E O L G U N O
L M U E S S O L O C
```

 PIZZA

 POMODORO

 FERRARI

 OLIVES

 GELATO

 VOLCANO

 COLOSSEUM

 GRAPES

Football 3

The Rome football manager wants to pick a team using players with shirts that are in the 3 times table. Can you circle all the shirts below that he would need to choose?

Find all the 3s

3

8

7   6   9   11

21   8   12   10

17   20   15   16

calcio
(cal-chee-o)
football

Football 5

The Milan football manager wants to pick a team using players with shirts that are in the 5 times table. Can you circle all the shirts below that he would need to choose?

Find all the 5s

5	6		
9	10	15	12
20	21	25	23
30	42		
45	52		

Design your own football shirt:

Pasta Sauce !!

A chef is getting ready to make lots of pasta sauce!

He needs 10 of each ingedient.

Looking at what he already has in his cupboards, can you work out how many extra he needs to buy to make 10?

 + = 10

 + = 10

 + = 10

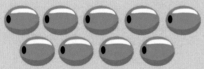 + = 10

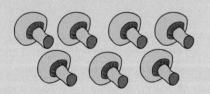 + (blank) = 10

il pomodoro
(eel pom-or-doro)
tomato

aglio
(al-ee-o)
garlic

il basilico
(eel basilico)
basil

funghi
(foon-gi)
mushrooms

olive
(ol-ee-vay)
olives

16

Pasta Squish !

Just as the chef is about to make his sauce,
he trips and drops his ingredients.

Lots get squished.

Can you work out how many he now has left of each?

10 - = ☐

10 - = ☐

10 - = ☐

10 - = ☐

10 - = ☐

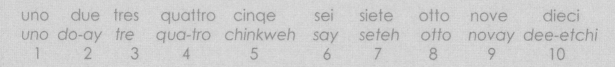

uno	due	tres	quattro	cinqe		sei	siete	otto	nove	dieci
uno	*do-ay*	*tre*	*qua-tro*	*chinkweh*		*say*	*seteh*	*otto*	*novay*	*dee-etchi*
1	2	3	4	5		6	7	8	9	10

Shopping until you drop!

Milan is a city in Italy that is famous for fashion houses - places that make beautiful handbags, shoes and clothes. There are lots of shops in Milan so it's a great place to buy a new bag.

You only have a €20 note and you want to buy two bags.
In each example below, can you circle the second bag you would be able to buy with it? Both bags must add up to €20.

Spend 20 Euros!

15 + 10 OR 5 = 20

10 + 10 OR 12 = 20

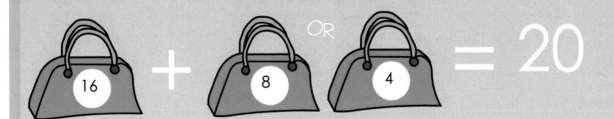

16 + 8 OR 4 = 20

7 + 18 OR 13 = 20

How much left?

These ladies are shopping for shoes!

If they start with a 20 Euro note and buy the pair of shoes, how much will they have left? Write it in the white box.

Any change?

 20 -  €14 =

 20 -  €10 =

 20 -  €19 =

 20 -  €5 =

Pizza Party!

It's time to throw a pizza party. Can you help the pizza delivery driver through the maze to pick up the pizza?

Pizza was first made in a town called Naples. When the Queen Magherita paid a visit, they created a special pizza for her, called Pizza Margherita.
You will still find this pizza on every Pizzeria menu.
Some say it is still the best!

Find the pizza!

Pizza Sudoku

There are many toppings you can put onto a pizza.
Can you complete this "pizza toppings" puzzle with tomato, mozzarella, olives and salami?

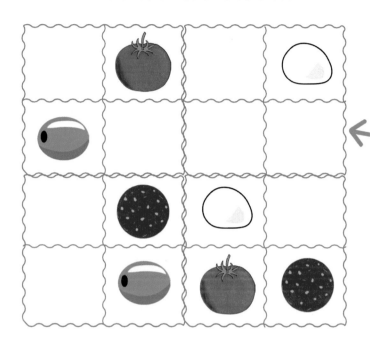

Fill in the gaps

Each item must appear ONCE in every row and every column, so think carefully...

What's your favourite pizza topping?

Pizza Making

You have to make 3 pizzas. Each one has to have the same amount of ingredients on it. Can you count and share out the ingredients below equally?

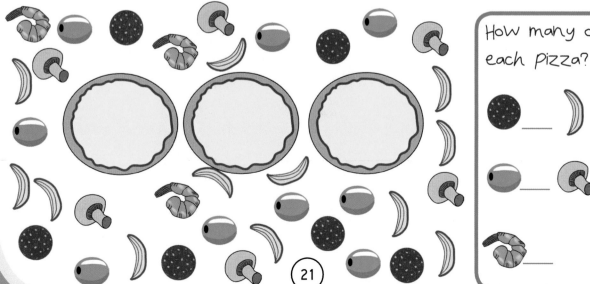

How many on each pizza?

 ___   ___

 ___   ___

___

21

Lake Garda Spot the Difference

Italy has two very large and famous lakes, Lake Garda and Lake Como - both in the north of Italy near to the mountains.

Lake Garda is the biggest lake in Italy.
Can you spot the 5 differences between the two lakes below?

spot the differences

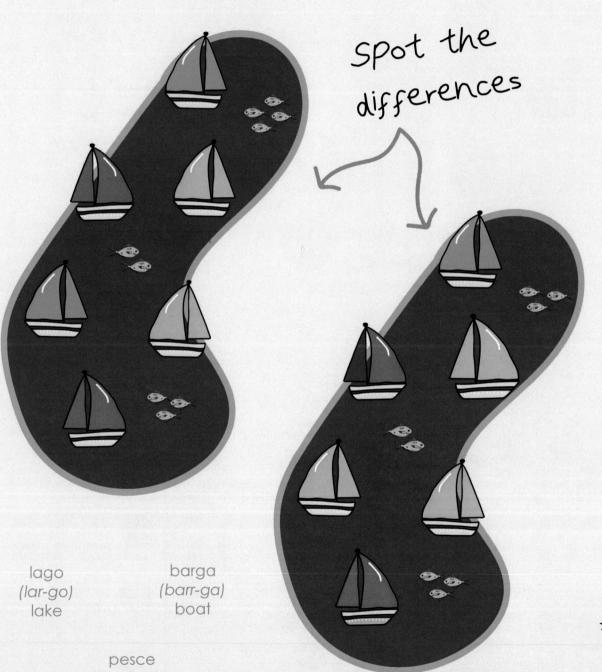

lago
(lar-go)
lake

barga
(barr-ga)
boat

pesce
(pesh-eh)
fish

Conundrum in Venice

There is a city in Italy called Venice that is mostly under water!
To get around you have to go by boats (called gondolas) which are pushed along using long oars.

In the puzzle below, can you match the clues with the correct gondola and gondolier (driver)? Read the descriptions on the pieces of paper carefully.

Match the description with the gondola

Carlo
1. Loves stripes
2. Got a new yellow top last week
3. Has a blue gondola

Pietro
1. Loves a matching hat and neckscarf
2. Has the same colour gondola as Carlo

Raphael
1. Has the same hat as Pietro
2. Has a red gondola
3. Has the same colour neckscarf as Carlo

The Leaning Tower

In a town called Pisa there is a famous bell tower that looks like it's falling over. It started to lean when they were building it but they made it safe and now it is one of the most famous buildings in Italy........but it still leans!

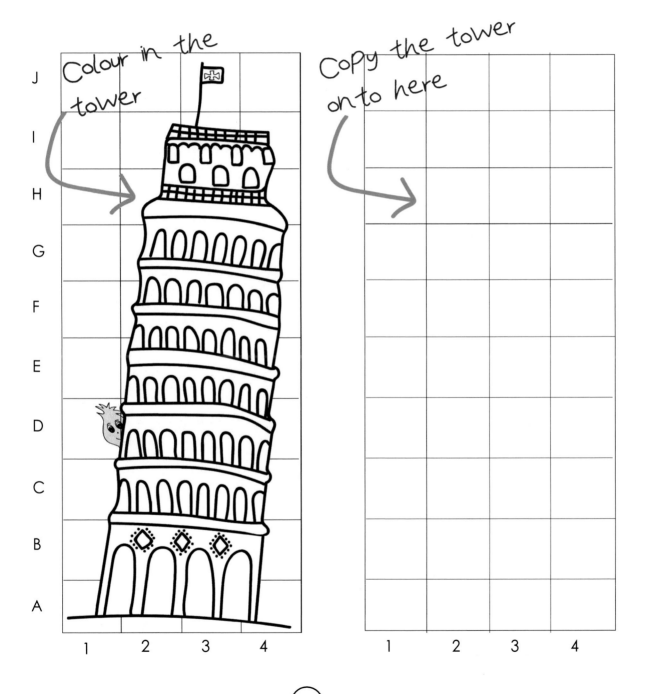

Colour in the tower

Copy the tower on to here

24

Roma and The Colosseum

The capital city of Italy is Rome. Or "Roma" in italian.
Rome was built over 2,000 years ago and its first ruler was a man
called Romulus - a boy who was raised by a wolf!

The Colosseum is one of the most famous ancient buildings in Rome.
It was used as a fighting ring for gladiators which the Roman
Emperors loved to watch. You can still visit the Colosseum and go
underneath it into the tunnels where the fighters used to keep tigers,
lions, elephants, giraffes and bears that were released through
trapdoors to join in the fighting.

Can you colour in this picture and add some of the animals
underneath that used to sneak up from the trapdoors?

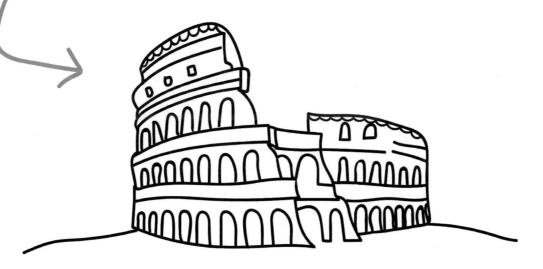

Romeo and Juliet

There is a famous love story set in Italy, where a girl called Juliet falls in love with a boy called Romeo. Their families are arch-enemies which makes it difficult for them to see each other but they sneak out to meet up and fall in love for ever after.

What do you think Romeo is saying to Juliet in this picture?

Romeo and Juliet

Colour this picture matching the colours opposite, and complete what you think they are saying to each other.

Colour and complete the speech bubbles

Mountains / Le montagne

Italy has many mountains and in the winter, you can ski or snowboard down them as they are covered in snow! The four highest mountains in Italy are Monte Bianco (4,808 metres), Lyskamm (4,527 metres), Monte Cervino (4,478 meters) and Grandes Jurasses (4,208 meters). Can you label the mountains below correctly according to height?

Which mountain is which?

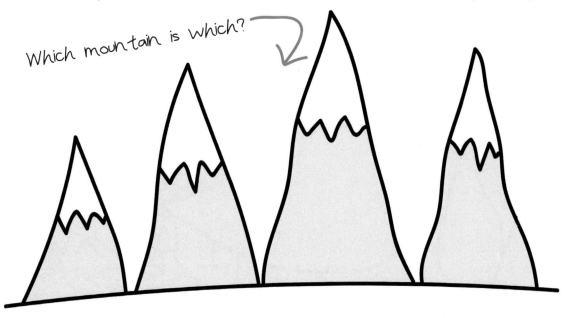

Can you decorate these snowpeople with faces and hats and scarves?

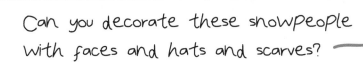

Mountains / Le montagne

After a morning skiing, you will be hungry! You might find some hot soup, a cheese fondue or a melted cheese sandwich to warm you up. Can you help these skiers, find their lunch?

Who is having what for lunch?

Italy shares mountain ranges with France, Switzerland and Austria so there is a good-choice of food available

Islands and Beaches

Italy has two main islands - Sicily and Sardinia. Both have beautiful beaches, and Sicily also has two live volcanoes - one of which is on a small island of its own. Can you help the sailboat below follow the directions and using the compass help it find its way to the correct island?

Go West 4 Places. Go North 3 Places. Go East 1 Place. Circle the island you arrive at. Happy sailing!

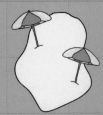

Start here and follow the directions

Gelato!

At every seaside town in Italy, you should be lucky enough to find a gelateria - an ice-cream shop! You will be wowed with the amount of flavours to choose from.

Can you find all the matching pairs and the odd-one out?

Find the odd one out

Decorate these ice-creams with your favourite toppings:

What is your favourite flavour of gelato?

_____

(31)

Volcanic Action!

Italy is home to many volcanoes; and three are still live! They are all in the south of Italy; Mount Vesuvius, Mount Etna and Mount Stromboli.

Volcanoes are formed when the earth's crust cracks and lets out some of the boiling and bubbling hot magma and steam underneath it.

Check out the picture below and copy the colours and labels onto the opposite page.

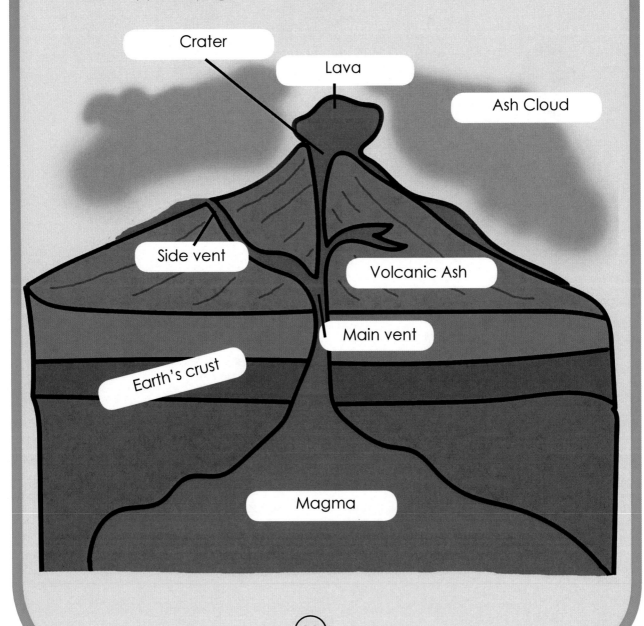

A buried city!

When Mount Vesuvius erupted in 79AD, there was so much ash and rock thrown out of it that a whole city got completely buried. Pompeii (Pom-pay) is the famous buried city but it has now been discovered and you can visit it!

Colour and label this volcano picture

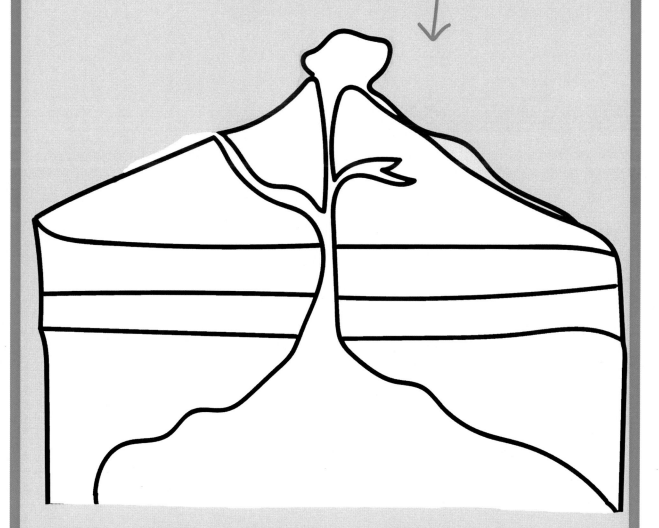

What do you think it would be like if a volcano erupted today?

Olive Groves

In many of the fields around Italy, you will spot rows and rows of olive trees. Olives are grown to eat on their own, or to squeeze to make olive oil which is used in lots of yummy Italian dishes.

Can you work out the repeating patterns in the rows of olives below? See if you can complete them:

Colour in the blank olives using the patterns for clues...

Do you like olives?

Ferrari Fever!

One of Italy's most famous cars is the Ferrari.
They are sports cars known to go very very fast.
They're built in a factory in a town called Maranello in northern Italy.

Can you measure each of the Ferraris below? The factory owner needs to know how long each one is? The bottom three haven't been painted yet - can you design the paintwork for them?

Measure up

Design your own

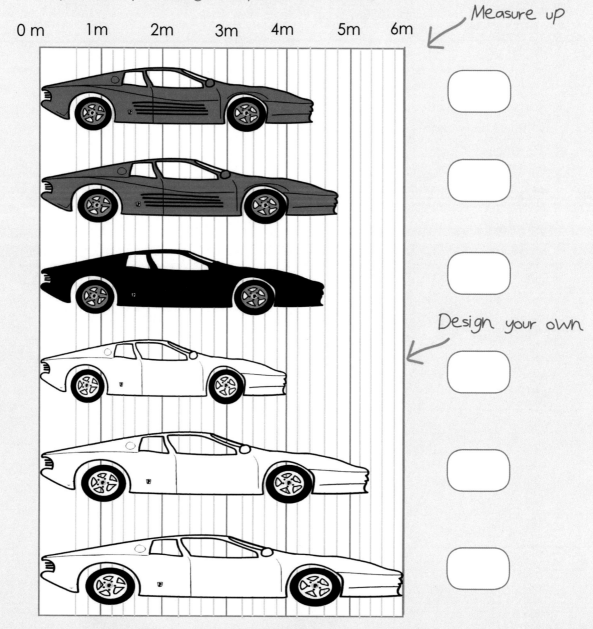

Quiz

How much do you think you know about Italy?

Answer these questions to find out... the answers can be found in this book! Good luck! Buona Fortuna!

In which town would you find this famous leaning tower?

_____

Can you name 3 popular pizza toppings?

_____

Can you name at least one of the volcanoes in Italy?

_____

What is this kind of boat called?

_____

What is the name for tomato in Italian?   _____

What is the tallest mountain in Italy called?

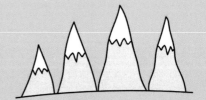

_____

Memory Bank

It's time to write down all the things you've done, seen and tasted on your trip!

WRITE, DRAW, STAPLE, STICK

A Place to Stay

Where are you staying in Italy? Is it a hotel?
A house? A chalet? An apartment? Something else?

Can you **draw a picture** of it here?

Home Sweet Home

Can you **draw a picture** of where you live back at home?

What is different about this and your holiday home?

What have you eaten?

Draw some food you have eaten on holiday on the plate below. What was your favourite?

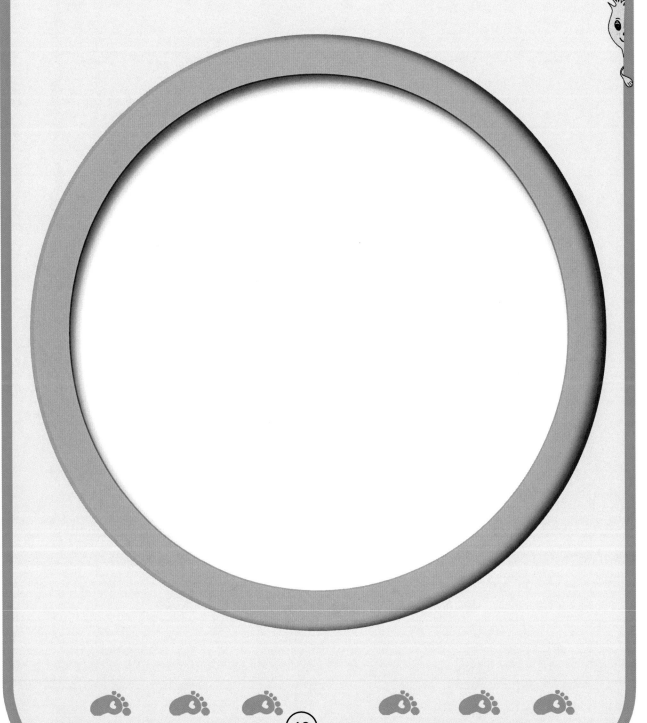

What adventures have you had?

Write a postcard about your adventures, and design a nice stamp:

Cartolina Postale

Momento Board

Stick bits and pieces on these pages that you've collected during your trip; favourite tickets, receipts, leaflets, drawings...

 # Daily Diary

Note down some of the different things you have done each day:

Monday

Tuesday

Wednesday

Thursday

Friday

Saturday

Sunday

Memory Gallery

Draw pictures or doodles of any special memories:

The Good and The Bad

Time to think about the best bits and the worst bits:

The best three things

The worst three things

Chitter Chatter

Talk with your family about these questions to help fill in the gaps:

Something I did for the first time:

Something I want to tell everyone when I get home:

Something that made me laugh:

Something I did that was brave:

Something I want to do again:

Index
(what's in this book and where you can find it)

All things Italy

Key skills

Memory making

Arriverderci

(goodbye, until next time)

I hope you enjoyed your adventure and completing this book along the way.

How many times did you spot me?

_____

Keep safe!
Love from
Topher xx

Where would you like to go next?

Spain

USA

Greece

France

Egypt

China

UK

Australia

South Africa

Thailand

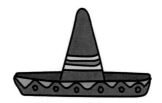

Mexico

Finland

Made in the USA
Las Vegas, NV
28 November 2021

35538343R00031